Hidden Dove
by ANN TUBBS

DEVOTIONAL SERIES
Part 1

Freedom *by* Grace

A 30-Day Journey into Galatians

ANN TUBBS

All rights reserved. This book is protected by the copyright laws of the United States of America. This book may not be copied or reprinted for commercial gain or profit. The use of short quotations or occasional page copying for personal or group study is permitted and encouraged. Permission will be granted upon request.

Scripture quotations marked TPT are taken from The Passion Translation. Copyright © 2014. Used by permission of BroadStreet Publishing Group, LLC, Racine, Wisconsin, USA. All rights reserved. www.thepassiontranslation.com

Scripture quotations marked NIV are taken from the Holy Bible, New International Version, Copyright c 1973, 1978, 1984 International Bible Society. Used by permission of Zondervan. All rights reserved.

Scripture quotations marked NASB are taken from the New American Standard Bible, Copyright c 1960, 1962, 1963, 1968, 1971, 1972, 1973, 1975, 1977, 1995 by The Lockman Foundation. Used by permission.

Scripture quotations marked KJV are taken from the King James Version.

Cover and book layout designed by Westerly Creative Studio.
www.westerlycreative.studio

ISBN: 978-1-7331253-2-1

ENDORSEMENTS

The freedom that accompanies life in the Spirit is something that every believer was created to walk in. Freedom from our own self-righteousness, and freedom to live life unhindered by the pains of the past. Paul's letter to the Galatians unpacks what this freedom looks like, and "Freedom by Grace" is a wonderful walk through this transformational epistle. Longtime friend and HIM leader, Ann Tubbs, offers a spiritually sensitive perspective on Galatians as she leads you through a month of deep personal encounters with Abba God.

Each entry unravels yet another layer of His heart for you as Holy Spirit brings healing, strength, and new joy through each step of the journey. "Freedom by Grace" will help you to recognize the Lord's voice with greater clarity, as you discover the invaluable gems of truth found in Galatians. Ann's prophetic voice and insights translate seamlessly into the devotional exercises and personal applications. This is a truly refreshing book that will lead you to experience a deeper measure of the infinite love of God!

Dr. Ché Ahn
President, Harvest International Ministry
Founding and Senior Pastor, HROCK Church, Pasadena, CA
International Chancellor, Wagner University

Have you ever felt like you could never quite measure up or that you needed to work harder for God's approval? This wonderful little devotional is a beautiful tool that will set your heart free. My dear friend, Ann is experienced in leading hundreds of people to a deeper intimacy with the Father. She has created a beautiful little devotional which takes scriptures from Galatians, her own devotional thoughts, meditation and application that will break you free!

Candice Simmons
Passion & Fire Ministries

My dear friend, Ann Tubbs, has written a beautiful, life-giving book that will allow you to lay hold of the truth that sets us free. As you meditate on the words of Srcipture, supported by the wisdom that Ann passes along, you will experience the love and acceptance of our Father God like never before. I highly recommend this book.

Stacey Campbell
Be A Hero
www.beahero.org

Ok, I am Ann's husband. The truth is though, she is the real deal. I have watched her grow in every way, especially in freedom. Ann has tried a lot of inner healing, but memorizing and meditating on the living word has brought incredible break through. These pages are full of nuggets for an inner life filled with the Spirit. These exercises are from experience and not just ideas. The devotional is a gift from the Lord to minister to your life.

Mark Tubbs
Transformation of the Nations Co-Founder
HIM Missions Apostle

CONTENTS

7	INTRODUCTION
11	**DAY 1:** GOD'S PURPOSE FOR ME
13	**DAY 2:** JESUS, OUR SACRIFICE
15	**DAY 3:** THE SPIRIT OF SONSHIP
17	**DAY 4:** CURSES ARE BROKEN
19	**DAY 5:** TEMPTATIONS OF RELIGION
21	**DAY 6:** PURPOSE OF THE LAW
23	**DAY 7:** THE FAITH OF JESUS
25	**DAY 8:** DESTINY
28	**DAY 9:** RECEIVING GOD'S LOVE
30	**DAY 10:** HIDDENNESS
32	**DAY 11:** GOD'S PERFECT TIMING
34	**DAY 12:** SLAVERY VS. SONSHIP
36	**DAY 13:** THE TWO COVENANTS
39	**DAY 14:** OVERCOMING THE SLAVE MENTALITY
42	**DAY 15:** GOD USES WEAKNESS
44	**DAY 16:** "FLOWING THROUGH YOU WITH MY POWER"
46	**DAY 17:** CHERISHING FREEDOM
48	**DAY 18:** THE POWER OF FATHERHOOD
50	**DAY 19:** OUR TRUE MOTHER
52	**DAY 20:** LITTLE LIES
55	**DAY 21:** THE FLOW OF LOVE
57	**DAY 22:** GOD TREASURES YOU
59	**DAY 23:** CRAVINGS OF THE SELF-LIFE
61	**DAY 24:** INTENSE CRAVINGS OF THE SPIRIT
63	**DAY 25:** INHERIT THE KINGDOM REALM
65	**DAY 26:** THE FRUIT OF LOVE
67	**DAY 27:** FRIEND OF SINNERS
69	**DAY 28:** STAYING IN YOUR LANE
71	**DAY 29:** GOD'S DELIGHT
73	**DAY 30:** WONDERFUL GRACE OF JESUS

INTRODUCTION

As a kid, I loved going to church. It felt like home. I loved the songs, the people, the kid's programs, the purpose it gave me in serving and the support when I needed it. As a pastor's kid, I sought to serve the church. And as a pastor's wife, I was thrilled to continue doing so. I did it all: directing choir, leading the youth, women's groups, cell groups, mission trips and endless other projects. I loved it all, especially the accolades that came with it.

I remember one evening at an appreciation banquet, we were all instructed to put notes in a bowl stating who we were thankful for. My name was mentioned by at least half of the people! And I felt so satisfied with myself. It seemed that I was a star of my own show!

Yet God, in his faithfulness, had a different plan for me. Praise God that he didn't allow me to stay in that place of pride and self-sufficiency. He created the perfect storm, or as I call it, " a severe mercy." I had believed in the lie that I had to work as hard as I could and to be as needed as possible to feel good about myself. It all felt so right--"serving" God, and serving people. But I didn't really know God.

When my husband and I were blessed with three children in two years (yes, I had twins), I quickly reached an end to myself. I took the role of motherhood very seriously and felt the extreme responsibility to be "everything" for my kids, while I continued to be "everything" for the church. After not sleeping more than an hour at a time for 7 months, I crashed. My body and mind were shutting down—I couldn't stop shaking, I had a hard time processing thoughts, and I was battling depression. Praise God! I couldn't perform anymore.

So began my journey to find God in a new, more tangible way. I finally learned my extreme need for Him, and I was desperate to know Him beyond the tasks and duties. I remember closing my eyes in my little Baptist church and telling Jesus, "I wish I could just see you. I wish you didn't seem so far away."

My desire to know him better started unfolding when we went to a Vineyard conference in Anaheim in the mid 90's. When the worship team began, the Presence of God was thicker than I had ever felt before. I leaned into Him and began worshiping with all my soul. Then I began "seeing" visions with my mind's eye—it was Jesus dancing with me! I knew it was an answer to prayer and much more real to my heart and spirit than just my own imagination. I was deeply touched and greatly encouraged that God had heard my heart's cry to see Jesus in a more intimate way.

From that point on, I was changed. I could no longer do "church" for myself, or even for others. I had to know God intimately and serve him the way he directed. I knew I needed to learn to hear his voice and continue to learn the ways of the Spirit to effectively follow him, so I read every book on the prophetic and dialoguing with God that I could find. I attended more Holy Spirit and prophetic conferences than I can count, I searched the Scriptures about hearing his voice, dreams and visions--and I was soaring in his love!

Yet, every time I left church, worship, and anointed fellowship, I still struggled with so much condemnation. Finally, I heard the Lord say, "Memorize Galatians!" I hadn't done any memorizing since I was a kid, and being in my mid-50's, wasn't so sure my brain still worked that way. But after a couple years of plugging away at it (yes, I'm pretty slow), I eventually had the whole book not only in my head, but also infiltrating my heart. I noticed that my thoughts were becoming more healthy—I loved myself more, I received God's grace so much more quickly and I was able to stop the constant condemnation I had always battled. Galatians taught me to let go of the people-pleasing and religious performance that was wearing me out. The best part was knowing that I was pleasing to the Lord and he had done everything to make me that way.

This is my desire for you. This workbook leads you through many prophetic, inner healing and deliverance exercises that are similar to what the Lord has led me through the last 20 years. Enjoy the process—it takes time to learn to think and feel different about God, about yourself, and about life. You might want to repeat this book several times and allow the Holy Spirit to go deeper in you each time. Every time I proofread this workbook I found new revelation and deeper healing of my soul. Enjoy this journey of knowing true freedom in God. Bless you much as you proceed...

– Day 1 –
GOD'S PURPOSE FOR ME

"But when God called me by his grace; and in love, he chose me from my birth to be his." (Gal. 1:15, TPT)

You were God's idea. Long before you were conceived, God planned for you. Eph. 1:4 beautifully says, "He chose us to be his very own, joining us to himself even before he laid the foundation of the universe!" (TPT)

He knew how many hairs you'd have on your head, He knew what nation and what parents you would inherit. He knew the struggles and pain you'd feel, the joys and talents to be developed, and He is delighted in you. He always loved you, even as an unborn thought. He was always proud to be your Papa.

Each of us has a purpose. Jeremiah's and Isaiah's purpose was to become prophets (Jer. 1 and Is. 49), for Paul—an apostle (an ambassador for the Kingdom of God), for you....? You may not yet be clear on the entirety of your purpose, but you can be assured that the same, good God that foreknew Paul, Jeremiah and Isaiah designed you to bring Him pleasure, to accomplish His will, and to enjoy Him forever.

Yet, the question remains—will you agree that you were a good idea? Are you willing to trust that God will ultimately use the pain and heartache you've been through for your good and His glory, and redeem all that the enemy has stolen? Will you trust that you have a purpose in this life that only you can fulfill? Will you believe His word that you are "wonderfully and fearfully made?" (Ps. 139) It will take some time to understand everything (some things not until we get to heaven), but choose this day to embrace the life God has given you. Learn to trust Him, that He will bring the dark, hard things around in its time.

What do you like about yourself? What do you enjoy doing? What unique qualities do you have? Take the time to appreciate yourself and to thank the Lord for making you so unique. What do you like about God? How did He make you like Him? You can use the space below to write your answers.

Join me thanking the Lord for making you:

Father God, I believe you are a good Father—that You created me with a purpose and You enjoy helping me grow and take pleasure in being my Father. Lord, forgive me for not always trusting You with my purpose and value; forgive me for not appreciating who You made me to be. I choose today to believe that You have set me apart as Your special daughter/son. I love You, God. Thank You for making me who I am and for the opportunity to have a close relationship with You.

As I listen for the voice of the Lord for you, this is what I hear:

"My beloved child. I have loved you before the foundations of the world. You have been in My heart always and I'm excited about who you are. You are My favorite one. I know this seems impossible to human thinking, but My love is so immense that I am able to focus on you and pour out this love to you as if you were the only one I created. I would still send My Son as a sacrifice for you alone. Allow My love to go deeper into your heart and bring healing to your soul. Rest in this place of acceptance and purpose."

- Day 2 -
JESUS, OUR SACRIFICE

> *"I pray over you a release of the blessings of God's undeserved kindness and total well-being that flows from our Father-God and from the Lord Jesus. He's the Anointed Messiah who offered his soul as the sacrifice for our sins! He has taken us out of this evil world system and set us free through our salvation, just as God desired."*
> *(Gal. 1:3-4, TPT)*

Because we are born into sin and into a fallen world, we know that we "aren't good enough" for God. So we may try to be better, to perform well, or to work really hard to feel better about ourselves. Yet, deep down, we know we can't make ourselves perfect, or righteous: "For the scriptures reveal and it is clearly obvious, that no one achieves the righteousness of God by attempting to keep the Law." (Gal. 3:11 TPT)

God loved us so dearly, that He offered His perfect Son as a guilt offering in our place. It is necessary for us to understand that his sacrifice for our sins is enough for our salvation and there is nothing we can add to it. Paul pleads with the Galatians to let go of their self-efforts of circumcision and Jewish regulations to make themselves holy (...you're acting as though Jesus the Anointed One is not enough. Gal. 4:2 TPT)

We do the same thing today. We may not be following strict Jewish Law, but we add our own rules to make us feel better about ourselves. Letting go of these self-made benchmarks takes humility, ("Surely, there is enough good in me to impress God.") When we finally come to terms with the fact that we can never please God with our own righteousness, we are then willing to admit that Jesus is our only answer.

Let us put our full trust only in Jesus' sacrifice for us and not in our sacrifice to Him.

Today's spiritual exercise:

1. Ask the Holy Spirit for ways you still rely on your own righteousness or strength to become "good enough" for God.

2. As you use your anointed imagination, look for Jesus on the cross. Walk up closely to Him at the foot of the cross. As He looks down at you, confess ways that you have tried to be independent from Him or self-sufficient in your own goodness. Confess your self-efforts and striving as sin (missing the mark). Repent of any other sin from the Holy Spirit's conviction.

3. Look at His eyes of love. Hear Him say, "I forgive you. Now, let me cleanse you."

4. Allow drops of Jesus' blood from the cross to permeate your mind, your mouth, your heart, your hands and your feet by faith. Receive His righteousness.

5. Look at how beautiful He made you to be and give Him praise.

6. Worship Jesus for His sacrifice, His love, purity, kindness, endurance, unrelenting devotion to you.

Hear these words from Jesus today:

"My dear one, it was worth all the pain and suffering for a relationship with you. I endured the misery of the cross for this everlasting joy of having you forever. You are worth it to Me. You are My priceless reward. Learn to see your perfection through My eyes, for My blood has made you righteous. There's nothing you have to do but to receive this gift of sanctifying love. This love will transform you more and more until that day I return for My perfect bride."

- Day 3 -
THE SPIRIT OF SONSHIP

"And so that we would know for sure that we are His true children, God released the Spirit of Sonship into our hearts—moving us to cry out intimately, "My Father! You're our True Father.""
(Gal. 4:6, TPT)

It may be difficult to come close to a Heavenly Father because of so many ungodly earthly role models. Our hearts may have become accustomed to feeling independent, abandoned or even abused verbally, emotionally and physically. This can be described as an "orphan heart", which makes it a challenge to trust Father-God.

God's answer for this was to send the Holy Spirit to comfort and heal our hearts. John describes it like this, "And I [Jesus], will ask the Father and he will give you another Savior, the Holy Spirit of Truth, who will be to you a friend just like me—and he will never leave you." (John 14:16, TPT) Savior, or parakletos in the Greek, means "one called to stand next to you as a helper." It would be impossible for us to have an intimate relationship with the Father without the Holy Spirit. He advocates for us, counsels, heals and comforts us.

It's important for a verse like Galatians 4:6 to be taken personally. It's the Father's heart to bring you intimately close to Himself. Therefore, He created you, redeemed you by Jesus' sacrificial blood, and then released His own Spirit to live inside you to heal, comfort and lead you closer to His heart.

The activation exercise for you today is a process. It can be done daily, for we are complicated and complex. Many of us have had years of bad habits, and we require a process of healing to undo faulty attitudes and beliefs. Be patient with yourself and trust that the Holy Spirit will transform your heart and mind in His timing, His way. Enjoy the process, and be filled with hope that intimacy with Father-God is our ultimate destiny.

Today's spiritual exercise:

1. Ask the Holy Spirit to come inside you. Breathe Him in by faith, (just as Jesus told His disciples to receive the Holy Spirit and then He breathed on them. Jn. 20:22)

2. Ask the Holy Spirit to show you attitudes and actions rooted from an orphan heart. (Example: Keeping God and others at a distance, not trusting Him, not being teachable or submissive to Him, trusting in your ability to sustain yourself, comparing yourself to others, clinging to people for security)

3. Ask the Holy Spirit to show you why you have chosen these ways. What is the root cause?

4. Forgive any parents, siblings, and spiritual authorities for ways they have failed you, and forgive yourself for your own failings.

5. Ask the Holy Spirit what He has to say about this subject. How does He see you?

6. Receive the Spirit of Sonship today. Thank Father God for His love.

Words from Holy Spirit for you today:

"I am at home in your heart. I love you and am proud to be your friend. I will never leave you or turn against you. My voice is gentle and loving. I will teach you how to stay close to your Father in heaven. I will teach you how proud We (Father, Son and Spirit) are of you. We are on a life-long adventure together, with never-ending joy, revelation, comfort and healing. When you go astray, I will steer you back into fellowship. Learn to trust My leading, precious friend."

- Day 4 -
CURSES ARE BROKEN

"Yet Christ paid the full price to set us free from the curse of the law. He absorbed it completely as he became a curse in our place. For it is written: 'Everyone who is hung upon a tree is doubly cursed.'"
(Gal. 3:13, TPT)

God is very serious about us knowing that our righteousness comes only through faith in Jesus. In fact, in Gal. 1:8 Paul declares, "Anyone who comes to you with a different message than the grace gospel that you have received will have the curse of God come upon them!" (TPT) And, "If you choose to live in the bondage under the legalistic rule of religion, you live under the law's curse." (Gal. 3:10, TPT).

If we allow ourselves to strive toward righteousness by keeping rules, then a curse of condemnation follows, because we ultimately fail every time. "Utterly cursed is everyone who fails to practice every detail and requirement that written in this Law." You can't live by two standards: one by complete freedom from condemnation only by the blood of Jesus, and one by trying to be good enough. The moment we put any faith into being good enough through rule-keeping, a curse of condemnation follows.

There are dozens of curses that come from condemnation. Here are some: sickness, barrenness, poverty, depression, death, futility, painful childbirth, turmoil, drought, slavery, mental illness, and robbery. Those curses are activated when we fail to practice the law.

But now we no longer have to put up with curses! We can break curses off our lives by faith in Jesus' blood, even when we haven't been perfect ourselves. If we who live by faith we are now holy, it's not dependent upon our performance. Jesus' perfection is constant and we can plead the blood of Jesus to break off every curse by faith! Just come to Jesus in a spirit of humility and repentance to break off these curses by His precious blood sacrifice for our sins.

Today's freedom exercise—breaking generational curses:

1. Thank the Lord for yourself, and your family line. What blessings have been handed down to you that you are grateful for?
2. What curses do you see repeated throughout your generations? (i.e. poverty, violence, rage, mental illness, adultery, alcoholism, perfectionism, religion, etc.)
3. Ask Holy Spirit who has participated in these sins in times past, including yourself. (father, grandmother, etc.)
4. Forgive anyone involved for participating in these sins. (Ex: "I forgive my grandfather and father for allowing a violent spirit to control them.")
5. Repent on their behalf and on behalf of your family bloodline for participating in these sins. (Ex: "Lord, I repent on behalf of my great-grandmother and myself for entering into adultery.")
6. Renounce participation. ("I renounce all participation with a poverty spirit from my family line.")
7. Break off curses and sins by the blood of Jesus. ("I break off a spirit of covenant-breaking from me and my family line, in the name of Jesus!")
8. Ask Jesus what He wants to give you instead. ("I receive a Spirit of Sonship, thank you, Jesus!")
9. Repeat these steps as the Lord gives you revelation.

Words from Jesus:

"My precious one, you are so valuable to me. I came to truly set you free. You can be the agent in your bloodline that frees generations. Don't give up. Even if you don't see immediate change, do not lose faith. There is indeed a righteousness that spreads to your whole family line as you come to me in faith and righteousness. The power of my blood to set generations free from strongholds is that powerful! Keep going!"

- Day 5 -
TEMPTATIONS OF RELIGION

If Jesus' blood is so powerful to conquer all sin and curses in my life, why to we go back to living under the law, or by our own self-efforts? I think most of us can relate to the mountain-top experiences of God's love, knowing our acceptance through faith in the finished work of the cross, only to find ourselves repeating similar patterns of performance and dead works which lead to condemnation.

Paul expresses great alarm as he begins chapter 3, "What has happened to you foolish Galatians? You must have been under some evil spell to have missed the revelation of truth. Didn't God open up your eyes to the meaning of Jesus' crucifixion?" (Gal. 3:1. TPT) He diligently taught his church the glory of living by faith in Jesus alone for salvation. Then, not so long later, they fall into a religious system of works. Why would they stray from the grace and provision Jesus offers?

One main reason is pride. We know we aren't perfect, but deep down, we find it hard to believe that our striving really counts for nothing. "Really?", "I'm not that bad of a person. I'm going to show the world that I can look pretty good." "If I just try my hardest, I know I can overcome." We try and do well for awhile, and we enjoy the accolades we get in those "successful" seasons. But we eventually run out of our own strength, self-control, or goodness, and we find ourselves losing our temper, being jealous of those more anointed, sleeping in through our quiet times, or falling back into addictions. And then, since our self-esteem relied on our success, the condemnation follows.

Another reason why we revert back to living in a religious system is peer pressure. We are communal people, made to be loved and to love. Rejection is never easy to endure. Many times our freedom from a list of rules causes others to back away from us in judgment. Our freedom can make others uncomfortable because they don't understand it and they don't want to be tainted by us. Some people would prefer us to be religious so they can maintain control of us to validate themselves. (Gal. 6:13 "...they push you to be circumcised so they can boast that you have become like them." TPT).

A third explanation for living by the rules instead of the power of the Spirit is control. Religion feels tempting to the one that doesn't want to fully surrender their will to God. It's much easier (so it seems) to make a list of do's and dont's than to give our complete trust to someone we can't control. That is why we have to know the true nature of our Father God. Galatians 4:8-9 is compelling: "Before we knew God as our Father and we became His children, we were unwitting servants to the powers that be, which are nothing compared to God. But now that we truly know Him and understand how deeply we're loved by Him, why would we, even for a moment, consider turning back to those weak and feeble principles of religion, as though we were still subject to them?"

Questions to ask yourself:

1. Which of these three reasons for staying in a religious system is most tempting for you? *(Pride in self-effort, fear of rejection, control...)*

2. Ask Jesus, "Why do I have a hard time with this? Write down your answer.

3. Ask Jesus, "How does this affect my relationship with you? With others? Continue writing what you hear the Holy Spirit telling you.

4. Repent of self-effort, people-pleasing, or fear of surrender. Ask the Holy Spirit to empower you to live by faith in Jesus' finished work on the cross, and not on your own efforts or the affirmation of others. Ask Him for the grace to more fully surrender to His control today.

– Day 6 –
PURPOSE OF THE LAW

"Why, then, was the Law given? It was an intermediary agreement added after the promise was given to show men how guilty they are! It remained in force until the Joyous Expectation was born to fulfill the promises given to Abraham." (Gal. 3:19, TPT)

It would be a reasonable question to ask why God didn't save Himself a lot of time by avoiding the Law altogether and going straight to the cross of Jesus. Why did He allow so many generations to struggle trying to keep all the laws of Moses? Because He knew the heart of man. As previously stated, we tend to think, "We've got this." "I don't really need a savior, I'll just try harder."

The Law leads to failure, which leads to guilt and condemnation. Look at it in your own life. When you're feeling smart, courageous, and self-righteous, are you motivated to surrender your whole life to God and lean on Him wholeheartedly? No, it's more likely that we give our whole selves to Him when we are desperate, when we feel there's nothing good in us, and when we're powerless.

That's what the Pharisees lacked. They thought they were able to fulfill the Law, and that's why Jesus had to take them to task by saying, "...and whoever says, 'You fool,' shall be guilty enough to go into the fiery hell." (Mt. 5:22, NASB) Who hasn't done that? God wanted us to know how powerless we were to be righteous in His sight. He wanted us to receive the gift of His Son instead of going around Him. "The Law, and our failure to keep it becomes a gateway to lead us to the Messiah so that we would be saved by faith." (Gal. 3:24, TPT)

"Be holy, as I am holy" is a command, yes, but it's obvious

we can't fulfill it on our own. He knows that. But what a beautiful invitation to receive His holiness as ours. What if He said, "Try to be a good person"? There's no standard, no provision to achieve goodness. Yet, that's how many of us live. Instead, let's surrender our goodness, and lack thereof, to God. Then, receive an impartation of holiness that comes through the power of His blood. Only through his provision we can begin to "Be holy, as I am holy." Praise God for our failures which leads to His victory!

Activation:

1. Name an area of your life where you struggle with sin or lack faith.

2. Thank the Lord for the failure in this area which shows your great need for Him.

3. Allow yourself to feel the pain of failure in this area. (Like wearing muddy clothing.)

4. Envision Jesus holding you in His white robe. By faith, watch the mud come off your dirty clothing and be absorbed into Him. Now both of you are wearing white.

Jesus Says to You Today:

"Don't worry about cleaning yourself up before coming to Me. I purchased your dirty rags. Now I wash you clean as snow. No amount of effort on your part can make you feel this pure. I give you pure gold. Your heart is as a rare and precious diamond, which reflects the character of your Father. That is what I see when I look at you, My beautiful, radiant one."

- Day 7 -
THE FAITH *OF* JESUS

We think that we chose Jesus, but Jesus chose us first. We think we put our faith in Jesus, but Jesus' faith brought us to that point. Paul writes, "We know full well that we don't receive God's perfect righteousness as a reward for keeping the law, but by the faith **of** Jesus the Messiah!" (Gal. 2:16, TPT. Emphasis added.) "You have all become true children of God by the faith **of** Jesus Christ! (Gal. 3:26, TPT. Emphasis added.).

Remember, it all started with God. God, before He made the world, had a plan to send you into the world to redeem you to Himself. (Eph. 1:4) To make this happen He sent Jesus into the world, who offered Himself as a sacrifice and through His faith called you to Himself. "It is the 'faith OF Jesus'", or what He believes about you, that makes you His very own.

Our faith waivers, but is tested and grows in maturity. Jesus' faith is constant. "Even if we are faithless, he will still be full of faith, for He never waivers in His faithfulness to us." (2 Tim. 2:13, TPT). He sees us from the beginning to the end and knows us through and through. He's not wondering if you'll make it, or if you'll finally become a better person. "You are found complete in the faith OF Jesus." It's a glorious thing to know Jesus has faith in me, that He sees where I'm going, that His faith has active power to sanctify and glorify me and unify Himself to me.

The more we live this Christian life, the more we understand it's a life of impartation, which is His life infused into ours--His faith, infused into our faith. That's why Paul writes, "I have been crucified with Christ, and it is no longer I who live but Christ in me;" (Gal. 2:20, NASB) We can rest in the knowledge that Jesus' faith is growing stronger in us everyday and we don't have to feel guilty about faulty faith anymore. The prayer of St. Patrick resounds in our hearts today: "...Christ with me, Christ before me, Christ behind me, Christ in me, Christ beneath me, Christ above me, Christ on my right, Christ on my left, Christ when I lie down, Christ when I sit down, Christ in the heart of everyone who thinks of me, Christ in the mouth of everyone who speaks of me, Christ in the eye that sees me, Christ in the ear that hears me. I arise today through the mighty strength of the Lord of creation."

Activation:

1. Ask Jesus for the things He has faith for in your life. Write them down as you hear them.
2. Forgive yourself for not having perfect faith. Ask Jesus for His faith.
3. In partnership with His faith, what big things can you believe for, not only in your life, but for others and the world?
4. Rewrite these lists as declarations using the faith of Jesus. (For example, "I declare that I walk in perfect love as Jesus' love flows through me!")

Jesus Says to You Today:

"You have only just begun to see what I will do through you. You are finally beginning to understand the power and glory that flows through you as we stand as one. I in you and you in Me. My faith is yours, and your weak faith is now made perfect in Me. See the end from the beginning through My eyes. There is nothing too difficult with Me. Just stay in this place of faith that I've provided for you. Just stay...with Me. I love you."

- Day 8 -
DESTINY

"My name is Paul, and I have been commissioned as an apostle for the Lord Jesus Christ. You need to know that my apostolic authority was not granted to me by any council of men, for I was appointed by Jesus, the Anointed One, and God the Father, who raised Him from the dead." (Gal. 1:1, TPT)

Paul is confident of his calling. He received it directly from both Jesus and the Father. It is clear that Paul's calling was to be an apostle to the Gentiles, and Peter's was to the Jews. (Gal. 2:7 "...seeing that I had been entrusted with the gospel to the uncircumcised, just as Peter had been to the circumcised..." NASB). It is also clear that God, through his grace, made both Peter and Paul successful as apostles. (Gal. 2:8 "for He who effectually worked for Peter in his apostleship to the circumcised effectually worked for [Paul] also to the Gentiles." NASB) God called them, commissioned them, and worked through them to make them effective.

But are Paul and Peter more special than you and me? If it's true that God shows "no partiality" (Gal. 2:6), does the Father and Jesus have a commissioning for us as well? Is there a specific call on our lives, and will He also work through us to make us effective? The answer is "yes!" That's why Galatians 6:4 is so motivating: "Let everyone be devoted to fulfill the work God has given them to do with excellence, and their joy will be in doing what's right and being themselves, and not in being affirmed by others."

So how do we know what our calling is from the Lord? Galatians 6:4 is a key to realizing it—what has the Lord told you to do, and what are you passionate about? What gives you joy even when others don't understand? We may not experience the intense visitations the way Paul did, but God does speak to all His children. (John 10:16)

When I really want to hear God clearly, I worship Him as I focus on His loving and faithful nature. I allow the Holy Spirit to enter my mind and heart and ask Him to "guide me into all truth (Jn. 16:13)." As I worship the Lord, I keep a notepad close and write down any revelation the Lord shows me. For instance, as I sing "Reckless Love", (by Cory Asbury, Caleb Culver, and Ran Jackson--Bethel Music), I notice what emerges into my spirit: "Before I spoke a word, you were singing over me..."(I see myself teaching groups how to get closer to God),..."You have been so, so good to me"...(I want leaders to be encouraged and feel loved),..."Before I took a breath, You breathed your life in me..." (I wonder how so-and-so is doing). After I worship, I survey my notes and I write down: teaching intimacy with God, encouraging leaders, pastoring people, intercession." This is just some of the callings God has given me to do. As I pursue these areas of ministry, through the Lord's guidance, I witness fruit in my labor and the maturing of my gifts and callings.

Try this exercise for yourself:

1. Worship with familiar, anointed music. Focus on the goodness of God. ("10,000 Reasons" by Matt Redman is also an excellent song about God's character.)

2. Ask the Holy Spirit to flood your mind and heart and guide you into truth about your destiny and calling.

3. Write down the things that come to mind. If some of them are your to-do list, that can even bring you revelation.

4. Do you notice a pattern to the things you think about?

5. Begin pursuing the things God gives you a heart for. Allow yourself room to grow and mature and don't give up. God promises to complete His work in you! (Phil. 1:6)

The Father's words for you today:

"My beloved child, I created you for a purpose. Your most important purpose is to be close to Me and that brings Me much joy. I have created you with specific desires, skills and anointing. As you move forward in obeying the things I nudge you to do, you will discover those things make you feel alive. Don't allow "failures" and and disappointments to steer you away from following these desires and passions within you. There will always be things to overcome, but as long as you don't quit, I will cause you to be effective by the power of My Spirit. I love you so much, My precious."

– Day 9 –
RECEIVING GOD'S LOVE

Paul's main goal was to know God's love, as declared in these amazing statements: "For love completes the laws of God (Gal. 5:14, TPT), and, "The only things that matters now is living in the faith that is activated and brought to perfection by love." (Gal. 5:6, TPT) The same is true for us.

It all starts with love. God's love leads us to faith. God's love shows us our blessing and inheritance, and God's love provides a way for oneness with Him. If we aren't good at receiving His love, it's difficult to understand any of His benefits, especially grace. We naturally go back to living by "shoulds" and "have to's" if we can't be drawn and propelled by a constant stream of His love.

Yet, it may not always be easy to access this kind of love. Our parents and others may not have been good examples of godly love. Our hearts have endured a fair amount of rejection, abandonment, condemnation, fear and abuse. We grow up thinking that God is like our imperfect parents, siblings and leaders so our hearts often grow numb, seared or hardened. It's difficult to experience God's love with calloused hearts. That's why we need the Holy Spirit to release healing to us.

God's love is expressed through His Spirit. That's why the fruit of the Spirit (love, joy, peace, patience, kindness, goodness, faithfulness, gentleness and self-control) is "love in all its various expressions" (Gal. 5:22-23, TPT). Through His Spirit, we can experience His joy for us, feel His peace comforting our hearts, and understand how patient He is when we fail. We receive His kindness, believe His goodness, lean on His faithfulness, and hear His gentle words all through the love and power of the Holy Spirit.

The Holy Spirit reveals the "great magnitude of the astonishing love of Christ in all its dimensions. How deeply intimate and far-reaching is His love!" (Eph. 3:18-19, TPT) But to start that journey of love, we must choose to want it, know it, feel it, and to live by it.

It's not always easy to start this journey of receiving love. When God finally said to me, "Will you let me love you?", I had a hard time. I was fearful that I couldn't live up to this love...that I would disappoint Him if I let Him in that close. I didn't yet realize that He was never disappointed with me and that my failure to love Him back couldn't stop Him. After a long, restless night, I woke up the next day and relented to His unfailing love. "OK, God, I'll let you love me, even though I don't really understand it yet!" That was the best decision I've ever made.

Ways to grow in receiving God's love:

1. Tell God you will allow Him to love you fully. Be honest about your fears.

2. Write this question, "Lord, how do you feel about me?" Write down what you hear.

3. Tell God what you love about Him.

4. Make it a habit to meditate on a modern version of Song of Songs (The Passion Translation, by Brian Simmons is especially intimate). He has an anointed way of expressing the love of God through this book. Here is an example:

    SS 1:5b "I feel as dark and dry as the desert tents of the wandering nomads. (us)" "Yet you are so lovely--like the fine linen tapestry, hanging in the Holy Place. (God)" (TPT)

    "My child, I know your inability to fully receive My love at this point, but I will heal your heart and teach you how I see you. Everyday I will release more revelation into who you really are in My eyes. How I love you with an everlasting love. Keep coming closer."

– Day 10 –
HIDDENNESS

> *"God's grace unveiled His Son in me so that I would proclaim the message of 'sonship' to the non-Jewish people of the world. After I had this encounter I kept it a secret for some time, sharing it with no one. And I chose not to run to Jerusalem to try to impress those who had become apostles before me. Instead, I went away into the Arabian Desert for a season until I returned to Damascus, where I had first encountered Jesus. I remained there for three years..."*
> (Gal. 1:16-17, TPT)

Saul (later Paul) had an amazing chain events in his life: while severely persecuting the Christian church he was struck blind and encountered Jesus. Then after receiving healing through a first-generation decisple, he was led to the Arabian Desert to receive amazing revelation from God Himself. Instead of being sent out immediately with incredible knowledge of the end times, throne room encounters, and spiritual insights, Paul was required to stay in the desert 14 years, with no public recognition.

Walking out our destinies always involves different seasons of testing. One of the important seasons is learning to remain "hidden." Just like Jesus was led into the desert after his baptism, so was Paul. And so will we.

We, like Paul, need time to soak in the Lord's presence so we can be established in His truths, His love, and His validation. Paul went from impressing the Pharisees, to becoming a "nobody" in the eyes of people. Since God wanted to be his main source of affirmation and identity, he allowed Paul to remain anonymous 14 years before he entered into the established church scene of Jerusalem.

Give yourself time for God to lay His foundation of love and truth in you. Yes, it is important to be a part of the church family and learn from church fathers and mothers, but seasons alone with God are essential. I spent years worshiping by myself in our church sanctuary and often wondered why more people didn't join me. Now I'm so grateful for that season because God was able to establish Himself more deeply into my heart and secure me to Himself. Many will be jealous of your time and may not understand this kind of love connection between you and Him.

If you are in a season of hiddenness, where others do not validate what you are doing, learn to praise the Lord. Tell him that He is enough for you, even if you never get recognition from man. Notice attitudes that arise, i.e., "I'm alone, nobody appreciates me, when will my ministry grow?," or, "Nobody knows my worth, I can't do this anymore!" Acknowledge the feelings that come during this season of hiddenness and discuss it with God. He knows what's inside of us. He wants to be our source of love, strength, validation, and hope. Thank him for this season alone with him. There will be a time when you wish you had it back!

Words from your loving Lord:

"Listen, my dearest darling, you are so beautiful—you are beauty itself to me! Your eyes glisten with love, like gentle doves behind your veil. What devotion I see each time I gaze upon you. You are like a sacrifice ready to be offered. When I look at you, I see how you have taken my fruit and tasted my word. Your life has become clean and pure, like a lamb washed and newly shorn. You now show grace and balance with truth on display." (Song of Songs 4:1-2, TPT)

Read these words again, as the voice of Jesus goes directly to your heart. Receive it with faith. Read one line at a time and let His affirmation of you go deeper, strengthening your hidden, secret relationship with Him.

– Day 11 –
GOD'S PERFECT TIMING

> *"When we were juveniles we were enslaved under the regulations and rituals of religion. But when that era came to an end and the time of fulfillment had come, God sent His Son, born of a woman, born under the written Law." (Gal. 4:3-4, TPT)*

As I have mentioned before, God could have released His plan of salvation through Jesus much earlier, but He knew the perfect time His people would be ready. We can see through history how God's plan unfolds. It seems that God loves the process and enjoys the journey with chosen ones. God loves juveniles, and yet, he doesn't leave us there.

Paul describes the system he was in as a Pharisee, following the law, as juvenile. They did the best they knew at the time with the law that was given. Then at the right time, when God knew it would be most effective, He released a better covenant. "Yet, all of this was so that He would redeem and set free all those held hostage to the written Law so that we would receive our freedom and a full legal adoption as His children." (Gal. 4:5, TPT)

If you have grown up in a legalistic, religious environment, don't begrudge it. Thank the Lord for the process of getting you ready for a new level of freedom. Thank Him for building in you that desire for a better covenant, a deeper freedom, closer intimacy and understanding of Sonship. People learn best when they have a felt need to know. What a gift hunger and longing can be. Following rules and regulations as a child and juvenile can be satisfying for a while, but in our lives a "time of fulfillment has come" so that "we would receive our freedom and full legal adoption as His child."

We may not yet fully understand what all this means, but we

are ready for something different. We want more. Cry out for more of God: more revelation, grace, and more understanding of adoption as His children. If you feel the stirring of the Spirit in this cry, a time of fulfillment has come to you! "Seek and you shall find."

Let's pray this prayer together:

Lord, I want more. I'm grateful for my upbringing which has led me to this desire. Thank You for all the ways You've revealed Yourself to me through the years. But, Lord, I know there's more. I thank You for stirring this hunger in me to know You more, to know who I am in You. Come, Lord Jesus, come anew today. Fulfill this longing. I will praise Your name forever.

Now listen for his response. Let the Holy Spirit rest on you and wait on Him. Look for Jesus' eyes in front of you. Stay still for at least one minute and let Him communicate to your Spirit.

As you stand in front of Him, allow your heart to be penetrated by his love. Perhaps you feel a burning love growing inside you. Listen for His words.

These are the words I hear:

"You are ready for more. My love is consuming parts of your heart that have been hidden for such a time as now. The fear is subsiding, and I am making you as bold as a lion. I will make you faithful to the end, and I will fulfill My purposes in you."

– Day 12 –
SLAVERY VS. SONSHIP

"Now we're no longer living like slaves under the law, but we enjoy being God's very own sons and daughters! And because we're His, we can access everything our Father has—for we are one with Jesus Christ!" (Gal. 4:7, TPT)

The opposite of living like a slave is living like a son or daughter. It's no fun being a slave. Webster describes it as this: "a person who is the legal property of another and is forced to obey them." Or, "work excessively hard without proper remuneration or appreciation; a person who is excessively dependent upon or controlled by something." As as slave, you have no rights, you can't build an inheritance, self-esteem is low, life is drudgery and duty, there's no sense of family or belonging, you are constantly under the control of someone else.

That is what being a slave to sin or religion feels like. We get stuck in patterns we feel we have no control over. Here's some examples of a slave mentality: "Why am I raging? Why can't I give this up? I have to work as hard as I can all the time. That person seems so much better than me!" These thoughts are all symptoms of slave mentality instead of a "sonship" mentality.

We can overcome all slave patterns by learning how how precious we are as God's sons and daughters. Through intimacy with the Father we can know how completely loved and accepted we are by Him. This enables us to overcome negative thoughts and slave mentalities. His words of affection eradicate negative thinking and as His own Spirit lives inside us, we are changed from the inside out! God released the Spirit of Sonship into our hearts—moving us to cry out intimately, "My Father! You're our true Father." (Gal. 4:6, TPT)

How does a child of God think? "Oh Father, I know I just judged that person. Forgive me...thank You for Your cleansing. I know I'm pure in Your eyes now. What are your thoughts for that person?" Or, "Father, I can't seem to overcome this anger. What should I do?" (Listen for his forgiveness and affirmation after we confess our sin, and allow the Father to show us the places in our hearts that still need healing, then allow the Holy Spirit to minister to those places.) See the difference? It feels like a relationship. The guilt doesn't linger. God takes you through a process of maturity, yet you are continually accepted in the journey.

Activation:

1. Ask the Holy Spirit if there's something you feel lingering guilt about?

2. Now ask the Father how He feels about that sin/weakness.

3. Place that guilt and condemnation, like in a package, in His hands. What does He do with it?

4. Now, what does He want to give you instead?

The Father's Words to You:

"Child, you are mine. I have known you from the beginning of time. Nothing you do or say surprises me. I knew what I was in for when I created you, and I am thoroughly delighted in you as my son/daughter. Do not fear My rejection. I know you completely and love you completely. It will take some time for you to absorb this, but for today, trust that My love and affection are the basis of our relationship. I will slowly unfold all you are to Me as my son/daughter over time. Enjoy the journey!"

- Day 13 -
THE TWO COVENANTS

"Tell me, do you want to go back to living strictly by the Law? Haven't you ever listened to what the Law really says? Have you forgotten that Abraham had two sons; one by the slave girl, and the other by the freewoman?" (Gal. 4:21-22, TPT)

In Galatians 4, Paul discusses two covenants. He compares the slavery of living by the Law to Ishmael, who was the son of Abraham's slavewoman. Isaac was the "son of the freewoman," namely Sarah. Although both sons were legitimately Abraham's sons, one was born into slavery and one born into freedom. Ishmael did not come into Abraham's inheritance. "He was a child of the natural realm. But Isaac, the son of the freewoman, was born supernaturally by the Spirit—a child of the promise of God!" (Gal. 4:23, TPT)

The first covenant is described as the natural realm. That's why living by rules and regulations come naturally. It's what we see with our natural eyes and measure physically. Ishmael was a result of Abraham's lack of faith. He tried to fulfill the promise of God by his own understanding and strength. A lineage of slavery followed.

The second covenant was God's miracle answer to His promise to Abraham. Isaac was born of the Spirit, while he was 100 and his wife 90! It wasn't about Abraham's ability or wisdom. It was about Abraham's faith...faith in a God who fulfills promises, to whom "nothing is impossible."

Like Abraham, we also choose to live either by the natural realm, or the realm of the Spirit. Let's say you've heard the Lord tell you that you are to be a prophet to the nations, or a powerful businessman like Joseph. In a slave or natural orientation, you might wonder how you could ever be enough. "Where would I even get the resources to go to other nations, or, build that business? I'm not sure if I hear from God clearly enough, I'm not as powerful, or smart as so-and-so." Or you would rely on your own strength: "I have to work 18 hours a day from now on!", and, "If it's to be, it's up to me!" These are all symptoms of living in the first covenant—depending upon yourself to fulfill promises.

In contrast, a person who knows their position as a son or daughter is secure in their Father's words. They know it's by aligning with their Father's resources, wisdom, revelation, and power that brings about the miraculous and fruitfulness. It's a new covenant of freedom with God as he carries the heavy load and opens the right doors.

Like Abraham partnered with God through a lifestyle of faith, we are also called to partner with Him. We are still called to walk through those doors as we learn to obey the Lord, step by step. God does what we cannot do and God calls us to do the things he instructs us to do. A spiritually-minded person who believes promises of fruitfulness will believe these things: "I'm going to do my part by studying in school, and work hard while having faith that God will give me the divine appointments wisdom needed to build a powerful company.", or, "My daughter seems so lost, but I believe God forgives my mistakes—He will teach her how to walk in His peace. I will continue to love her with My Father's love." So, yes, we have a part in fulfilling God's promises—just like Abraham had to walk out a lifestyle of faith. But the new covenant provides a supernatural fruitfulness beyond what we deserve, or can make happen.

Questions for today:

1. What has God promised you?

2. Have you tried to fulfill it on your own strength and wisdom? Or, have you refused to walk through a door open to you because of fear of failure or shame from the past? Confess this to the Lord.

3. Ask the Holy Spirit to cleanse your mind of natural thinking; ask Him to instill the faith of Jesus in God's ability and not yours.

4. Ask the Lord if there's something specific He wants you to do, or believe for. What's the next step of faith?

- Day 14 -
OVERCOMING THE SLAVE MENTALITY

"Expel the slave mother with her son! The son of the slave woman will not be a true heir—for the true heir of the promises is the son of the freewoman." (Gal. 4:30, TPT) These words came out of Sarah's mouth to Abraham. Although Abraham was distressed about the thought of casting out Ishmael, God confirmed Sarah's words: "...for through Isaac your descendants shall be named." God did not forsake Ishmael, as he also made him a great nation. Yet, it was through Isaac's descendants that the supernatural was released and eventually led to Jesus' birth.

There comes a time that we must "expel the slave mother and her son" in our own lives. This is an active, deliberate process. We can learn to recognize ways that a slave mentality affects us--from its futility and negativity, to the self-depreciation and self-reliance. God's ways are higher with a world of endless possibilities, profound belonging, and empowerment.

We must learn to expel doubt, self-effort, fear and loneliness, and we must be militant in our determination to have a transformed life, according to God's truth. In addition, we need to recognize that there are spiritual forces behind the slave mentality.

Learning to walk in Sonship (and "Daughtership") will attract resistance. (Gal. 4:29) Our mind wants to go down familiar rabbit holes of doubt and fear where evil spirits come to oppose and oppress you. In fact, Jesus promised that His followers will be persecuted. It takes a commitment to be transformed from slavery to sonship.

Here are some effective methods of transformation:

1. Meditate on God's Word, especially verses about our identity as His children.

2. Resist negative thoughts of doubt, fear, and abandonment, taking every thought captive.

3. Learn from those of great faith and intimacy with God.

4. Saturate yourself in the Lord's Presence, learning to absorb His love more and more.

5. Repent of participating with lying, evil spirits and command them to leave your presence, in Jesus' name.

Just as Jesus declared to Peter: "Get behind me, Satan! You are a stumbling block to Me; for you are not setting your mind on God's interests, but man's!" (Mt. 16:23, NASB), we can also use the authority Jesus gives us for freedom against the attacks of the enemy in our life- "Get behind me, Satan, and all your cohorts, you will not cause me to feel like a slave, but I choose to follow the ways of God and walk in His truth!" "Jesus...gave the disciples authority over unclean spirits, to cast them out...." (Mt. 10:10). We can follow this example and expel spiritual forces against us:

Spiritual exercise for today:

1. Name a doubt or fear, or feelings of abandonment that you face regularly. (i.e. "I'm insignificant", "I'm waiting for the next shoe to drop", "Life is so lonely")

2. Ask the Lord for a verse or word that refutes that lie. (i.e., "You are the apple of My eye", "I will never leave you nor forsake you", "I know the plans for you, to give you a hope and a future.")

3. Repent for believing in the lie. ("I repent for believing my feelings more than Your Word", or "I repent for comparing myself to others.")

4. Renounce any spirits that would reinforce that lie. ("I command any spirits of insignificance, loneliness, and/or fear of failure to leave my presence, in Jesus' name!")

5. Ask The Holy Spirit to fill you. What does He want to give you instead?

God's Words to You:

"I have come to give you life, and life abundantly. You are just beginning to know My plans for you. Keep going toward My light and away from the death that surrounds you through negativity. I am coming upon you in a new, powerful way in this next season. Get ready for more, prepare your heart and mind for more! This is just the beginning!"

– Day 15 –
GOD USES WEAKNESS

"Beloved ones, I plead with you, follow my example and become free from the bondage of religion. I once became as one of you, a Gentile, when I lived among you—now become free like me...You are well aware that the reason I stayed among you to preach the good news was because of the poor state of my health." (Gal. 4:12-13, TPT)

Paul's health was suffering, his eyes were not doing well: "Some of you were even willing, if it were possible, to pluck out your own eyes to replace mine.!" (Gal. 4:15, TPT) We know that Paul didn't intend to stay in Galatia, but because of his ailment and weakness he had no choice.

Because Paul remained in Galatia, he was able to love them, teach them, exhort and live among the people there. Without his ailment, we would not have had this wonderful letter to the Galatians, showing us all how to become more free!

God allows each of us to endure weakness and hardship. We may begrudge it, whine about it, try to proclaim it away, but still God allows it. Paul may not have understood why he had to suffer this illness, yet he trusted in the Lord and was used powerfully where God had planted him.

Even as we mature in our character and faith, weaknesses yet prevail. God allows them in our lives to remain dependent upon him. It also creates a mutual interdependence with others. Paul expresses, "You were so kind to me, and did not despise me in my weakness, even though my physical condition put you through an ordeal while I was with you." (Gal. 4:14, TPT) The Galatians were obviously compassionate toward Paul, which opened their hearts toward him and enabled them to receive from him. So, Paul's ailment ended up being a great blessing to the Galatians, and to us.

Don't begrudge your weakness and need for others. God uses it. Of course, this doesn't include sin, because "Jesus released us from our sins by His blood." (Rev. 1:5, NASB) He sets us free of curse of sin, but sometimes our complete victory over it comes by leaning on the faith of others. Learn to thank God for your weakness. Allow others to give to you in your frailty, as we care for others in theirs. It takes humility to accept the fact that we won't ever be perfectly strong in every area here on earth. Yes, we are perfect in God's eyes and free from the stain of sin, yet He allows us to need each other, sometimes desperately.

Thank you, Lord, for using Paul's weakness to bless us all. Thank you for the message of freedom. You give us beauty for ashes!

Spiritual Exercise:

1. Name three weaknesses that you have. How do you feel about them?

2. Do you really believe that God can use those weaknesses for His glory? Listen for God's voice in relation to your weaknesses.

3. Learn to accept yourself—the strong and the weak. Do some self-talk of acceptance. For example: "Ann, I know you've struggled with inconfidence, but you are growing. You are teachable and this weakness helps you rely more fully on My power instead of yourself. It also helps you to remain humble and patient with others' insecurities. I love you, and I'm proud of you."

Words From God to You:

"My beloved child, I see your desire to obey Me. I know that you are disappointed with yourself at times when you feel that your actions and attitudes don't please Me. Learn to rest in My forgiveness. I'm not disappointed by your shortcomings. I love you as you overcome, as you learn to trust, but My love for you isn't dependent upon your growth or maturity. I'm the God of the broken, the downhearted, the hurting and the weak. Learn to receive My love even from that place. Then wholly lean on My strength to overcome temptation and fears. I will always be there for you."

– Day 16 –

"FLOWING THROUGH YOU WITH MY POWER"

"You are my dear children, but I agonize in spiritual 'labor pains' once again until the Anointed One will be fully formed in your hearts and become visible through your lives!" (Gal. 4:19, TPT)

Paul cared so deeply for the Galatians and their ability to live freely, he "agonized" over their state. He knew that he couldn't change them…it was a work of the Spirit.

There is such power in agonizing with spiritual labor pains. As we allow the Holy Spirit to express Himself through us, we find that He has such longing for us to come into the fullness Jesus paid for. Romans 8:23 describes it like this, "…We who have already experienced the first fruits of the Spirit also inwardly groan as we passionately long to experience our full status as God's sons and daughters—including our physical bodies being transformed" (TPT).

The Holy Spirit's longings inside us are a gift from the Lord. God loves us where we are, yet there's a groaning for more oneness with Jesus. The Holy Spirit is constantly drawing us to be more and more like Jesus, in Jesus, and by Jesus. This longing is not only for ourselves, but for those God gives us.

One of the most loving things we can do is allow the Holy Spirit within us to agonize for those we love so they can experience oneness with Jesus. How do we do this? We ask for a spirit of intercession to be released within us. We ask for God's love for the ones we are praying for, and we ask for the power of the Spirit's groanings to be expressed through us.

Many times in intercession the Spirit may express Himself through physical manifestations, such as groaning, tears, or birthing. Don't quench the Spirit at these times, because He wants to birth something through you. I remember when we were pastors of a local church in the mid 90's. It was common to see people "birthing" and groaning in the Spirit. We often wondered why God would do such a thing, and "is it really God?" Yet, the fruit of this birthing in intercession released much power through His Spirit: power for healing, joy, passion for Jesus, hunger for God, heavenly vision, miracles, and more.

God will birth by the power of the Holy Spirit through anyone that is willing. Ask Him for His heart for people, then yield to the movement of the Spirit within you. Maybe not everyone will understand, yourself included, but you will see the fruit and enjoy the communion with the Lord through it.

Spiritual Exercise:

1. Close your eyes and ask the Lord who He wants you to intercede for today.
2. Ask the Holy Spirit to fill you anew with God's heart for this person or region.
3. Allow the Lord's emotions to rise up within you.
4. Now, allow the Spirit to manifest through you. (Perhaps you'll speak in tongues, "birth", cry, laugh, groan, ache in your heart, even overflow with joy, or simply rest in peace).
5. Visualize what the Lord is doing and agree by faith.
6. Worship God for who He is.

Words From the Lord Today:

"My precious son (daughter), there is much I want to show you. As you make yourself open to the leading of My Spirit, you will find yourself entering into the agenda of heaven. I long to reveal My plans to My friends, but few are available to Me. Take the time to enter into this place of the Spirit-realm. I will teach you many things and release My Kingdom through your prayers. I love sharing My plans with you and flowing through you with My power."

– Day 17 –
CHERISHING FREEDOM

"Let me be clear, the Anointed One has set us free--not partially, but completely and wonderfully free! We must always cherish this truth and stubbornly refuse to go back into the bondage of our past!"
(Gal. 5:1, TPT)

Free,...completely and wonderfully free! Stubbornly refuse to go back! Paul is so emphatic to warn us to cling to this freedom. Our freedom from religion, law, our flesh, hell, curses, and oppression was paid for with a great price: the blood of God's Son.

It is all too easy to revert back into a slavery mentality—our flesh really likes the comparisons and man-pleasing, the do's and don'ts to make us feel good about what we can measure. Also, being part of a religious system can offer acceptance and accolades. It can be easier to live by what our natural eyes see and by others' affirmation and understanding than to walk by faith in God's pleasure of us.

Yet, freedom in the Spirit—nothing compares to that! It's wonderful to wake up feeling loved by your Father, to feel the warmth of the Spirit inside you as your constant Companion, to have the power to overcome sin and shame, to love others freely and fully, as well as yourself. This is what freedom in the Spirit brings.

How do we maintain this freedom in the midst of constant warfare that wants to bring us back into slavery? Gratitude. "We must always cherish this truth and stubbornly refuse to go back...." We must love freedom so much that when the enemy tempts us to feel condemned, or we seek to please men, or doubts and fears creep in, we can say, "No! I'm a precious daughter (son), God does not condemn me, but loves and accepts me."

And, "I love your Presence, Lord." Don't ever forget what Jesus has done for you.

Can you remember what it was like before you felt His freedom? Do you remember striving and fatigue, negative inner dialogue, finding no peace or rest? Tell the Lord how grateful you are for that chance to be free, to feel His love, to see life as an adventure in His hands instead of drudgery.

We tend to press on for the new thing, ask God to meet our needs, strive to know more and to be even freer. Yet, let's take the time today for thanksgiving. Let us never forget how far we've come.

Prayer:

Lord, we cherish the freedom you give us. We do not take You for granted; we are so grateful that you've called us out of a system that we could not win by winning the battle for us. Thank you for giving us Your Spirit to empower, comfort and heal us. Thank you, Jesus, for dying in our place to escape the punishment we deserve.

Activation:

1. Name 3 things the Spirit of God has helped you overcome. Thank Him for these things.

2. Name 3 people that have helped you come into a freer place. Thank God also for them.

Words from Your Heavenly Father:

"Yes, I have set you wonderfully and completely free. You have yet to understand the full meaning of that. Each day I can show you new ways to walk in My freedom. Think of it as an amazing love journey of joy and satisfaction. I feel your gratitude and I'm pleased with you. I'm grateful for you, also, that you have decided to go down this road of life with Me. I love you, my precious one."

- Day 18 -
THE POWER OF FATHERHOOD

Who's your daddy? Paul appeals to the Galatians that he is their father. "I write to you as your apostolic father..." (Gal. 5:2, TPT). He also reminds them of Abraham's fathering: "Abraham, our father of faith, led the way as our pioneering example." (Gal. 3:6, TPT) He goes on to say that "those who are the true children of Abraham will have the same faith as their father!" (Gal. 3:7)

Paul highly valued fatherhood. He "agonized" over his children, he appealed to fatherhood of Abraham's faith to be an example, and he was led to confer with the Jerusalem fathers--James, Peter, and John. He highly valued their affirmation of him: "I submitted to them the gospel which I preach among the Gentiles...(Gal. 2:2, NASB), "and recognizing the grace that had been given to me, James, and Cephas, and John, who were reputed to be pillars, gave to me and Barnabas the right hand of fellowship..." (Gal. 2:9, NASB).

God is our ultimate good Father, but He also gives us spiritual fathers here on earth. In fact, I believe we cannot come into the fullness of our destiny unless we are aligned with godly fathers. Paul could have ventured into missionary work without the affirmation of the Jerusalem fathers, but God wants His body to be one, and interdependent. Just as Paul says, "Follow my example", we also need examples to follow.

Yes, every spiritual leader has their faults and shortcomings, as does every natural father and mother. Does God do away with fathers and mothers because they're not perfect? He calls us to honor them, love and align with them. We align with Abraham's faith, we align with Paul's call to freedom, and we also align with the fathers and mothers God has given to us personally. That doesn't mean we agree with everything they say and do. (Paul confronted Peter about his hypocrisy). Yet, he esteemed Peter and the other apostolic fathers by seeking their counsel, confirmation and even commissioning. He wasn't a lone ranger, and he recognized spiritual authority. Because of that, his ministry was blessed by the Jewish churches of Jerusalem. He enjoyed the fellowship of godly men that had gone before him, and he learned to be a good father to the Gentiles.

What is your experience with spiritual authority? Does it make you feel squeamish and gun-shy, or excited, longing for more, and grateful? Many of us have had bad experiences with controlling or negligent leaders. We may need healing from the Lord to let go of the past concerning earthly fathers.. Don't allow a seared or wounded heart prevent you from aligning with the fathers and mothers God has for you today.

Activation:

1. Close your eyes and ask the Holy Spirit to show you any lingering emotional wounds you may have from your natural or spiritual fathers.

2. Pray this prayer of forgiveness: "Lord, I forgive my spiritual leaders,_____ and _____ for mistreating me in times past--not recognizing my value, or not loving me well. Don't hold those sins against them.

3. Repent for ways you have not been a good leader. (Ask The Holy Spirit to show you any faults you have had as a spiritual mother or father.) Receive His forgiveness and choose to forgive yourself.

4. Align your heart. Now, Lord, I submit my will to yours regarding spiritual fathering and mothering. Are there new alignments you have for me in this season? Show me how to align even better to the leaders You've given me.

5. Thank the Lord for those that have fathered you, and have been good examples and took you under their wings.

- Day 19 -
OUR TRUE MOTHER

"In contrast, there is a heavenly Jerusalem above us who is our true mother! She is the freewoman, giving birth to freedom."
(Gal. 4:26, TPT)

Webster's definition of mothering involves "bringing up a child with care and affection, to look after kindly and protectively, sometimes excessively so." There is no perfect mother, as many of us have struggled with some measure of neglect or abuse emotionally, physically, and mentally. Many mothers didn't receive the nurturing necessary to express the compassionate and tender heart of God that He longs for us to experience. Yet, our need for nurturing and care from the foundation of our lives to the time we leave this world is vital to our well-being.

The Bible actually has a lot to say about God wanting us to be mothered: "So many times I have longed to gather a wayward people, as a hen gathers her chicks under her wings..." (Mt. 23:37, TPT); "My father and my mother have forsaken me, But the Lord will take me up." (Ps. 27:10, NASB); and, "I am humbled and quieted in your Presence, like a contented child that rests on its mother's lap, I'm your resting child and my soul is content in you." (Ps. 131:2, TPT)

Not only does God mother us Himself, but He provides spiritual mothers within the church. When Jesus was told that His mother and brothers were waiting outside for Him, His response was "Who is My mother and who are My brothers?" Pointing to his disciples, He said, "Here is My mother and My brothers. For whoever does the will of My Father in heaven is My brother and sister and mother." (Matt. 12:50 NIV)

God also provides us with mothering through a "heavenly Jerusalem". In fact, Paul states that this is the source of true mothering. We know that there is a "cloud of witnesses surrounding us." (Heb. 12:1, NASB) and there are saints worshiping in heaven even as our spirits worship in heavenly Jerusalem. (Heb. 12:22-24) As we worship in His presence and glory, our spirits can begin to commune with these saints as we worship our King together. Knowing that there are those who have gone before us who are cheering us on as a cloud of witnesses can provide encouragement and support through the spirit realm in times of emotional need.

So, there is no reason to feel motherless and to remain with feelings of neglect, as God knows our deepest needs. He himself cares for our souls, he provides mothering through those that know Him and do his will, and He allows our spirits and emotions to commune with a heavenly family as we worship our King.

Listen for God's voice even today as he reminds you, "I will never leave you, nor forsake you. I am proud of who you have become and I will continue to heal your heart as you stay close to Me. Let Me gather you as a chick under My wing today. I love to hold you and I will never let you go!"

Spiritual Exercise:

1. Close your eyes and ask the Lord who He wants you to align yourself with to be mothered. (They don't have to be older). Are there judgments you made against your natural mother, or yourself as a mother that prevent you from doing this wholeheartedly? Confess and forgive your mother (and/or yourself).

2. Release false expectations of this person to meet all your needs and ask the Lord to help you receive from her what He intends to give you through this person.

3. Thank the Lord for this "mother." How can you bless and honor her today?

4. How can you "mother" someone today? (Even if you are a male, as Jesus did)

– Day 20 –
LITTLE LIES

"Don't you know that when you let even a little lie into your hearts it can permeate your entire belief system?"
(Gal. 5:9, TPT)

Small things are significant in the Kingdom of God as the tiny mustard seed grows to be a bush large enough to house many birds. So also, a little yeast permeates the whole batch of dough. Yeast can be both negative or positive in Scripture. In Matt. 13:33 yeast represents the Kingdom of God, while in Luke 12:1, it represents the hypocrisy of the Pharisees.

Just as Proverbs says "Do not despise the day of small beginnings", we must also allow Jesus to help us "catch the little foxes"--the little lies in the foundation of our belief system. If lies are given license to permeate our minds and hearts, they will infiltrate our attitudes about ourselves and God, and they will eventually lead us down a compromised lifestyle based on deception.

It's especially important to identify lies of legalism and religion as Galatians continually warns us against. We may think that some inward process of striving and performance is good for us, and that we should never feel too good about ourselves so that we will be "better" people. But that's not how God's mercy works. He declares us "not guilty" because of what He's done, not us. We can't allow any amount of self-effort to contribute to our righteousness, or right standing with God. Striving and independence from God do not bring forth good fruit in our lives. It leads either to condemnation, pride, comparison, exhaustion, jealousy, or defeat. If you feel these effects it's time to ask the Lord to root out every hidden lie that contradicts this basic truth: "Those who have been made holy shall live by faith." (Gal. 3:11) We must not tolerate any other source of righteousness in our thinking.

The following are common lies that the enemy tries to plant in the compliant minds of little ones. Perhaps, through circumstances you couldn't control or understand, you allowed the seed of some of these lies to take root, even as a young child:

1. I am on my own. I have to take care of myself.

2. If people really knew me, they wouldn't like me.

3. I am acceptable if I can please those in authority over me.

4. I am worth more if I'm successful.

5. My feelings are not important.

Spiritual exercise:

Ask the Spirit to search your heart. Ps. 139:1 "O Lord, you have searched me and have known me" (NASB).

As you ask The Holy Spirit these questions, write down the answers you hear:

1. What lies have I allowed in my heart? (write down one at a time)

2. Where did these lies start? (Forgive those involved with painful memories, including yourself.)

3. What is your truth in this area? (Here are some common truths from the Bible: "I have loved you with an everlasting love", "You have been made right through Christ", "I'm the author and finisher of your faith", "I call you friends", "I knew you before you were born and had a purpose for you", "The Father loves you like He loves Jesus.")

4. Soak in the truth of His words to you, until you feel deep peace in your heart.

Jesus' Words to You Today:

"You are My perfect one. I see you from heaven's perspective, and My words have already made you clean...and still, you are in process. You are sanctified and still being sanctified. Allow me to heal those places where lies about Me have hurt you. I am your Healer, your Friend, your Good Shepherd. I am forgiving and tender, with a fierce undying love for you. Will you believe these things rather than the whispers of lies that come from the pain?"

- Day 21 -
THE FLOW OF LOVE

"Demonstrate love to your neighbor, even as you care for and love yourself." (Gal. 5:14 TPT)

"Don't be selfish!" "Be nice!" We may have heard these words growing up. Or even, "Put God first, others second, and yourself last." Jesus' own words instruct us: "If you truly want to follow me, you should at once completely disown your own life." (Mark 8:34, TPT)

Yes, we are to lay down our lives in surrender to Jesus. That is not because of any self-rejection or self-disdain, however. We are not diminished to some lowly state of insignificance when we surrender our lives to Jesus. On the contrary, as we surrender to Him we are actually made truly alive in unity with Him. We don't become nothing, or dissolved, but more like our true self...or, perhaps, a Jesus-flavored self.

This is how we truly learn to love ourselves, others, and God. When we surrender our wills to Jesus and accept oneness with God as described in John 17 "that they may all be one; even as You, Father, are in Me and I in You, that they also may be in Us," then we can really learn to love. All love comes from God (1 Jn. 4:7). So, as we yield to this love-flow between God to us, it flows to others, and back to God. Love becomes like a cycle, and a river—first between the Father and Son, to us, and then to others... or, to others, and then to us.

If we stop this river of love by rejecting ourselves or diminishing our own value, it's like turning down the river valve of love in our hearts. Love gets diminished--we have less love to give others, and we experience less love from God. If we hold bitterness against others, this also diminishes the love-flow for ourselves and the Lord. That's why the two greatest commandments are the greatest: love God, love others as well as yourself.

Spiritual Exercise:

1. Think of someone you have difficulty loving.

2. Imagine a triangle of God, you and this person.

3. Allow the river of God's love to flow over you by faith. Let it wash down through you from the top of your head to the bottom of your feet, especially letting it fill your heart.

4. Now, imagine God pouring this same kind of love over the person you named.

5. Through the love God has for this person, look at them from God's perspective.

6. Ask God what He loves about them.

7. Ask Him what He loves about you.

8. Now allow that river of love from God to flow out of you to that person. Let any bitterness or hardness wash out with this love flow.

9. Thank God for putting this person in your life so you could learn more about His love.

10. Pray for that person.

Can you see how impossible it is to hate our brother or sister, or yourself, while flooded with the love of God?

God's Words to You Today:

"Don't try to love difficult people. You can't do it adequately through your own strength. Instead, let the love I have overflow through you to all those around. Then you'll find there is no room left in your heart for bitterness, or fear, and walls of rejection. I have come to give you life abundantly, especially in your relationships. You can walk in this abundance even now."

- Day 22 -
GOD TREASURES YOU

"But if you continue to criticize and come against each other over minor issues, you're acting like wild beasts trying to destroy one another." (Gal. 5:15, TPT)

Galatians 5:26 adds, "So may we never be found dishonoring one another, or comparing ourselves to each other, for each of us is an original. We have forsaken all jealousy that diminishes the value of others" (TPT).

Why is it so easy to see the negative in ourselves and others? Why do we often feel the need to compete with others, which leaves us feeling either prideful or discouraged? Even though we may know the importance of guarding our tongues, why do we still criticize and compare?

One reason we compete and compare is because of insecurity. We cannot give genuine affirmation and acceptance to others if we don't feel it ourselves. If we continue to be critical and judgmental toward ourselves, we can expect that critical spirit to come against those around us. If we are saturated in God's tone toward us and words of encouragement, it will overflow to all those around.

Notice how Jesus viewed people: Nathaniel was declared to be a man of "no guile"; Peter was named "the Rock"; and James and John were referred to as "sons of thunder." Jesus could have called Nathaniel a loner under the tree, or Peter a coward knowing he would deny Him; or James and John competitive and selfish for wanting to sit next to Jesus on the throne. But He didn't see his friends that way. Proverbs 19:11 states that "It is His glory to overlook a transgression." Jesus saw the gold in people.

God's heart for us is passionate. Psalm 139:17,18 expresses, "Every single moment you are thinking of me! How precious and wonderful to consider that you cherish me constantly in your every thought! O God, your desires toward me are more than the grains of sand on every shore! When I awake each morning, you're still thinking of me." God is constantly thinking of us and drawing us to Himself. As we receive and bask in His affection, we can afford to lavishly release this acceptance to those around us. We find it unnecessary to compete against others or to entertain thoughts of jealousy, for we know that we are uniquely cherished by our heavenly Father.

Activation:

Write down a way you feel judgmental toward yourself. Read Psalm 139:17,18 one more time. Allow God's words to go directly into your heart, one line at a time. Does the Holy Spirit want to whisper additional things into your spirit? Wait and listen. Do you feel the love and validation He gives? Allow his affirmation to overshadow your feelings of insecurity and weakness.

Now write down the name of someone you feel jealous of, or competitive with. Ask God to forgive you for allowing comparisons and envy to take root, then ask God for his eyes toward that person. Ask the Lord, "How do you see this person? What gifts have you given them? How do my gifts and strengths work well with that person's?" Write down what you hear or what comes to mind.

Give God thanks for sending that person into your life so you could become more like Jesus through this process.

God's Words to You Today:

"You are uniquely mine. There is no one that satisfies my heart like you do. I do not compare My children because each one has such a distinct purpose. As you learn to wallow in the warmth of My love and acceptance, you will learn that you are becoming more and more authentically you as the pretense and performance melts away. How I love you, My child."

- Day 23 -
CRAVINGS OF THE SELF-LIFE

"And what are the cravings of the self-life I'm referring to? They are obvious; sexual immorality, lustful thoughts, pornography, chasing after things instead of God, manipulating others, hatred of those who get in your way, senseless arguments, resentment when others are favored, temper tantrums, angry quarrels, only thinking of yourself, being in love with your own opinions, being envious of the blessings of others, murder, uncontrolled addictions, wild parties, and all other similar behavior." (Gal. 5:19-21, TPT)

Notice that the "covert" sins and the blatant sins as equally undesirable. Many have avoided murder and wild parties, but who hasn't loved their own opinion or been a little jealous of others' blessings? "The wages of sin is death"--all sin. But God has provided a different way of living: through the power of the Holy Spirit. One goal of Galatians is to convince each reader of their sin and their need for a savior. This is just as important for the highly disciplined, religious ones, as Paul had been. Galatians 3:22 declares: "But the Scripture makes it clear that since we were all under the power of sin, we needed Jesus!" (TPT)

Learn to appreciate the conviction of the Spirit. Sometimes we can feel that we're doing fine on our own, but God has a deeper cleansing, a higher road for us to walk. That's why it is so important to stay in the Word of God. Let God take you deeper into truth which brings even more freedom.

Often the Holy Spirit highlights a particular behavior or attitude that He wants to heal and transform, one at a time.

Activation:

1. Write down one area from this list from Galatians 5:19-21 that Holy Spirit wants to bring more freedom to.

2. Confess this sin; ask Jesus to pour his blood (spiritually) over that craving for complete forgiveness, and cleansing. Now, forgive yourself and let go of all shame attached to it.

3. As you read the list, other people may come across your mind. If you have pride ("At least I don't do that!"), confess the pride to God. Forgive them of their sins. Ask Jesus to forgive and wash them clean.

Jesus' Words to You:

"My precious one, my sacrifice was enough. I have purchased the penalty of your sin and you are free from all guilt related to those sins now. But don't trust yourself to live a righteous life. I know your flesh is weak, and I understand the temptations that you endure. Keep your eyes on me. As the triggers in life cause you to slip into unhealthy patterns of doubt, fear, and pride and you find your mind wandering from the truth, come to me. I will never shame or belittle you. I am tender and sensitive to the weak places of your heart and mind. Come to me. As you learn to take my hand when you're afraid and insecure, you will find that the life flow of my love and peace will strengthen you to overcome. Even when you don't think you will ever effectively resist the pull of the enemy, come to me. I have not come into the world to judge the world, but that I would bring you salvation--salvation in every area of your life. It will not happen all at once, but it will happen. Never stop coming to Me, and you will see how far We can go...together."

– Day 24 –
INTENSE CRAVINGS OF THE SPIRIT

"For your self-life craves the things that offend the Holy Spirit and hinder him from living free within you! And the Holy Spirit's intense cravings hinder your old self-life from dominating you! The Holy Spirit is the only One who defeats the cravings of your natural life. So then, the two incompatible and conflicting forces within you are your self-life of the flesh and the new creation life of the Spirit."
(Gal. 5:17, TPT)

One main goal in Galatians is to compel believers to quit striving for their righteousness. Paul wants to emphasize God's superior plan for living a holy life, a more effective plan than attempting to keep every rule and regulation. He sent us help from the inside out. The good news is that when we believe in Jesus as our savior, not only does His sacrifice enable God to forgive our sin, the Holy Spirit also lives within us: "And now God shows grace to all of us and gives us the promise of the wonderful Holy Spirit who lives within us when we believe in the Messiah. (Gal. 3:14, TPT) The Holy Spirit is not only a heavenly, omnipotent power, but He is a passionate, equipping person of the Trinity, making Himself accessible to us at all times.

Not every believer continues down a path of victory. God still gives us a choice to yield to the power of the Holy Spirit or not. That's why Paul says in Gal. 5:25 "We have now chosen to live in the surrendered freedom of yielding to the Holy Spirit!"

We have to ask ourselves what we really want? Do we want to continue a road of gossip and addiction, hatred and resentment, without much power and authority—a life to please our flesh? Or, do we want to live like Jesus—intimate and surrendered to His

Father continually, full of love, supernatural understanding and good fruit?

If the answer is communion with God and living like Jesus, the Holy Spirit can help us get there! It's going to be a process of maturing, but trust the Holy Spirit to convict, inspire, reveal, and empower. Lean on His intense desire to bring us to victory over every sin. Never settle for less.

Let's ask for more of Holy Spirit:

Holy Spirit, I honor You in my life. I ask You to fill me afresh today. Never leave me to my own ends, Holy Spirit. I want Your conviction, love, affirmation and power to live a mature life like Jesus did. Thank You for being my Friend, Helper, Inspirer, and Revealer of Truth. I choose to lean on You again today to overcome my own fleshly desires.

Spiritual Exercise for Holy Spirit Infilling:

1. Ask Holy Spirit to fill your mind. Keep receiving Him as He infiltrates your entire brain and head. You may feel His Presence and begin to become more light-headed. Or, you may feel nothing and receive His Presence by faith.

2. Ask Him to fill your mouth and give you prophetic utterance and wisdom from God in all that you say today. May the words of your mouth come from Him and bless all those around you.

3. Receive Holy Spirit to fill your heart. He is able to heal wounds and rejections. He is able to strengthen your heart's resolve. He can enable you to receive more of God's love. Wait on Him to work in your heart.

4. Ask Holy Spirit to spring up from your belly like rivers of living water today, refreshing and strengthening you as you live out every detail of this day.

5. Allow the Spirit to fill your legs and feet as He guides you into every step you take today. Holy Spirit, lead us out onto the path that will most glorify You.

- Day 25 -
INHERIT THE KINGDOM REALM

"Haven't I already warned you that those who use their "freedom" for these things will not inherit the Kingdom realm of God?"
(Gal. 5:21b, TPT)

The Kingdom realm of God! Isn't that what we all want—everything heaven has to offer: peace, revelation, new life, wholeness, healing, oneness with Jesus, glory, perfect fellowship, and angelic encounters? The amazing thing is that Jesus releases heaven on earth ("Your kingdom come, Your will be done, on earth as it is in heaven." Mt. 6:10 NASB) In addition, our spirits have already been raised with Christ and seated in the heavenly realms. (Eph. 2:6 and Col. 3:1) as we are made holy by the power of His blood. (Eph. 2:13, Heb. 12:23-24)

Our sins are completely removed when we choose Jesus' sacrifice for us. So, we can be immediately seated with Christ in the heavenly realms, chosen to rule and reign with Him. We may still be learning to overcome old sin patterns, but we are no longer devoted to a life of sin. The Aramaic literally means, "those who devote themselves to these things [sin] will never inherit the "Kingdom realm of God!"

Because you are made one with Jesus, you qualify for this Kingdom realm. Even if you've spent a lifetime of violence and bitterness, you can turn from those things, repent, receive forgiveness, receive fresh empowerment from Holy Spirit and continue living in His Kingdom realm continually, by faith.

2 Cor. 5:20 describes us as ambassadors of Christ. It's like living with one foot on earth, and the other in heaven. With one

turn of the head we can focus on one world or the other. Let's choose the life, love and power of heaven today.

Would you like to see and feel more of the Heavenly realms? *Follow these steps of prophetic sight by faith:*

1. Repent of any sin or unforgiveness, especially against yourself. Allow the Holy Spirit to release forgiveness and cleansing. Believe that you are made holy and pleasing to God.

2. Pray that Holy Spirit would fill your imagination with revelation from God. (Eph. 1:18 "I pray that the light of God will illuminate the eyes of your imagination, flooding you with light, until you experience the full revelation of our great hope of glory." TPT)

3. Use your anointed imagination to see a "Jacob's ladder", just like Jacob did with angels ascending and descending from heaven. (You can "see" with the eyes of your heart.)

4. By faith, allow your spirit rise higher and higher as you climb this ladder to a porthole going into heaven.

5. See Jesus at the top saying to you, "Come up here, where I am!" (Rev. 4:1)

6. As you get close to the top, let Jesus pull you through the port hole as he grabs your hand.

7. Now, spend time with Jesus in the heavenly realms. Let him hold you and tell you how much He loves you.

8. Ask Jesus to take you by the hand to see your Heavenly Father on the throne. (Rev. 4) as you walk with Jesus to the throne, worship Father God. Allow Him to pick you up as a child. Let Him tell you how much He loves you and how pleased He is with you.

9. Ask Holy Spirit to reveal Himself. What does He look like, what does He want to give you?

– Day 26 –
THE FRUIT OF LOVE

"But the fruit produced by the Holy Spirit within you is divine love in all its various expressions. This love is revealed through: joy that overflows, peace that subdues, patience that endures, kindness on display, a life full of virtue, faith that prevails, gentleness of heart and strength of Spirit." (Gal. 5:22-23, TPT)

As we learn to turn our face toward heaven, Jesus' love is continually poured into us like a river. Through knowing this kind of love, the fruit of the Holy Spirit flows freely through us in all His various characteristics: (love, joy, peace, etc.) Brian Simmons, of the Passion Translation has listed the fruit of the Spirit as action words, accomplishing something. For instance, we don't just feel kind, but kindness flows through us to benefit others. So, the fruit of the Holy Spirit not only benefits ourselves, but all those we are in contact with. This is how we become the "fragrance of Christ." (2 Co. 2:15, NIV) "For we are to God the pleasing aroma of Christ among those who are being saved and those who are perishing."

Those in the world have perhaps never tasted heaven until someone like us releases Jesus' scent (fruit) into the world. We can't conjure up this fruit by our own strength or will. That is why Paul emphasizes that following Jewish regulation cannot bring any eternal fruit. People are hungry for what only God can give. And we can only give it to them as we turn from our self-life and allow the Holy Spirit to flow and impart this fruit to us and through us.

Spiritual exercise:

1. As Jesus puts His hand on your heart, listen for Him to say, "I have loved you with an everlasting love." (Jer. 31:3 NASB)

2. Look for Jesus' eyes to penetrate into you as He says, "I am filling your heart with overflowing gladness."

3. Let Jesus embrace you as he whispers, "I leave the gift of peace with you—my peace. Not the fragile peace given by the world, but my perfect peace." (Jn. 14:27 TPT)

4. Holy Spirit flows through your body, washing away any anxiety or pride that makes you feel impatient.

5. Listen for Jesus' kind words for an area of discouragement in you.

6. Allow the virtue of Jesus to flow into you as you "touch the hem of his garment."

7. Jesus reminds you of His faithfulness to you. Thank Him for his steadfast love through all the seasons of your life.

8. God's voice is gentle, and Jesus' nature is meek. Hear the gentleness in his tone toward you today.

9. Holy Spirit releases His strength to you to continue down the right path today.

Jesus' Words to You Today:

"I don't expect you to have the fruit of the Spirit in your own strength. Many times you have tried to be kind or good, but have fallen short, bringing discouragement. Know that My blood has washed away all sin and discouragement. You are victorious through Me. I give you my very own Spirit to lead, and empower you forever. Learn to yield, and not strive. Learn to live free, led by my peace and acceptance at all times. Then you will truly be a fragrant vessel of My glory, and My love."

- Day 27 -
FRIEND OF SINNERS

> *"My beloved friends, if you see a believer who is overtaken with a fault and has fallen from the place of victory, may the one who overflows with the Spirit seek to restore him to fellowship with the Anointed One. Win him over with gentle words, which will open his heart to you and will keep you from exalting yourself over him."*
> (Gal. 6:1, TPT)

It's always painful to see the ones we love turn their backs to God. Our reactions can vary between dismay and anger, to judgment or even pity and tolerance. Yet, God offers us His wisdom in response. His heart is "humble and gentle" (Matt. 11:29) toward us, even when we're led astray. In fact, Rom. 2:4 reminds us that "the kindness of God leads us to repentance."

The Lord gives us the perfect solution for the times we are grieved over our estranged loved ones: 1. Notice the believer who has fallen; 2. Be overflowing with the Spirit in reaction to them; 3. Seek to restore him to fellowship with Jesus; 4. Use a humble approach and a gentle tone; 5. Don't view yourself as superior to him. This approach will open his heart to restoration. Sometimes it takes a process, both in the one seeking to restore (to maintain the right attitude), and the one being restored.

We must remember to avoid both extremes: being harsh and judgmental, or tolerant of sin and supportive of compromise. Jesus' response to the woman caught in adultery was the perfect example of Gal. 6:1. He was gentle, merciful and compassionate, yet invited her to a life free from sin. (Jn. 8:11) The old adage--"love the sinner, hate the sin" is still true and still effective, yet it takes the Spirit of God to accomplish it.

Spiritual Activation:

1. Ask Jesus to show you any harsh attitudes you may have toward someone in sin.

2. Invite Holy Spirit to fill you afresh; let Him pour His Presence into you until overflowing. Receive Jesus' perspective regarding this person.

3. Repent of any judgment or compromise you may have regarding the sins of this person. (Sometimes we are harsh with others because of our shame in a similar area of weakness.)

4. Lift up this person in prayer. Ask the Lord to forgive them and give them grace to repent.

5. Is there any action the Lord wants you to take in relation to this person (i.e.: write a note, give a gift, pray strategically, prophecy to).

The Lord's Words to You:

"My dear one, follow My instructions—seek to restore those around you to fellowship with Me. My Spirit will convict them of sin, you cannot do this. My Spirit will heal them of root causes for their failures—you do not fully know the cause yet Learn to be their advocate because they cannot yet hear Me in certain areas. I am a God of great mercy and triumph. Never doubt My ability to restore the gravest sinner and darkest situation. Know My light. Release the light of God through your prayers and acts of kindness. Never doubt My ability to turn the situation around for their good and My glory. I am the Friend of Sinners, and the Father of Lights. Learn to trust Me with your loved ones. Learn to believe and not doubt. Then I can truly use you in their lives for great miracles and reunion with Me."

- Day 28 -
STAYING IN YOUR LANE

"Let everyone be devoted to fulfill the work God has given them to do with excellence, and their joy will be in doing what's right and being themselves, and not in being affirmed by others."
(Gal. 6:4, TPT)

Joy in being ourselves, knowing that we please our Heavenly Father—isn't that what we all want? It may take a little exploration to find the work that is most fulfilling, but it is worth the effort. God has given each of us each specific work that only we can do in the way that He intends. Only you have the exact combination of experience, talent, creativity, skills, education and context that is needed for God's assignment for you. That's why it is pointless to judge how we are doing compared to others. No one can understand your longings and abilities like God does.

We can know that we are on the right track by the peace and satisfaction we feel in doing his will. We feel more "alive" when we are doing what He intended for us. We have the fortitude to keep going when things get difficult, and we feel the grace of God to push us forward. If we veer away from the "lane" God has given us, we can easily lose heart, become bored, or take on things that were not meant for us, which can lead to burn out. That's why it is so important to say "no" to the invitations that are not our assignment. If we fill our days with activity and relationships haphazardly, we may not have the energy and focus for the best and the most fruitful work.

When we sense God's pleasure in our work, we can do our most excellent work with joy. It is so satisfying to live our lives for an audience of one. Learn to look for His eyes of pleasure in you, and to listen for His voice of affirmation. If we do get off track, He is never harsh or judgmental but promises to give us wisdom and direction when we ask for it with faith.

Spiritual Exercise:

Allow yourself the grace of listening to God's pleasure about your work. Feel His pride in you as you read from Zephaniah 3:17: The Lord thy God in the midst of thee is mighty; he will save, he will rejoice over thee with joy, he will rest in his love, he will joy over thee with singing. (KJV)

Most of us are trying to fulfill multiple roles and various types of work. Listen for His affirmation as you read this passage again, using my paraphrase. Allow His Spirit to strengthen you and empower you to be excellent in every work the Lord has given you, through His excellence:

"I am your Lord as you carry out your duties of_____. I live among you and your loved ones as you work. I am your Savior in every area of your life, and I give you victory in your responsibilities. I am overjoyed with you...I love you so extravagantly. I am never critical of your work, and I never accuse you or shame you. It doesn't matter if you receive others' accolades if you listen for My joyous song over you."

Close your eyes and listen for His song over you, by the Spirit. Now, breathe in the strength and excellence of His Spirit. Ask Him if there are new directions He wants you to go.

- Day 29 -
GOD'S DELIGHT

"And all those who live in agreement with this standard will have true peace and God's delight, for they are the Israel of God."
(Gal. 6:16, TPT)

Paul is closing his letter to the Galatians by encouraging the believers to live by "this standard." "This standard" refers to the main themes written in this letter: righteousness by faith, adoption as God's loved children, living by the power of the Holy Spirit, pre-ordained destinies given by God, loving one another and self, God's grace, heaven's reality, and freedom from religious bondage.

As we learn to live by these principles, we are promised to experience true peace and to enjoy the knowledge that we are God's delight. Think of it—God's delight! What are you delighted in? Ice cream, grandchildren, Disneyland, vacations, a gourmet meal, a good piece of artwork, being asked out on a date, Christmas morning? Focus on that feeling of joy—hope arises with you, your heart may swell, you have a smile on your face, you contemplate the wonder of what you're experiencing, life seems pretty great. Now imagine God's delight in you with this same emotion, but multiplied a billion times stronger. If our hearts can delight over watching a little girl dance, imagine how strong God's joy can be watching you worship and enjoy His Presence? It brings Him far more emotion and passion than we've ever known. Choose to believe He feels this way for you as you live in His love, grace and power.

Paul declares that "we are the Israel of God." What did God feel about Israel? Israel was the "apple of his eye," or His "most precious possession." (Deut. 32:10, Zech. 2:8), "...He has sent me against the nations which plunder you, for he who touches you, touches the apple of His eye." (Zech. 2:8 NASB). God's saying, "Whoever messes with my kids will have to deal with me!" He's very protective and committed to each of His chosen ones. If you "live by this standard" of receiving the grace of God for your righteousness through Jesus' sacrifice, trusting the Holy Spirit to guide and empower you, you are truly God's delight and the Israel of God. What a privilege!

Spiritual activation:

1. Ask the Holy Spirit to enlighten the imaginations of your spiritual sight as you look for Jesus' eyes in front of you.

2. Tell Jesus that you love Him and worship Him from your heart.

3. Ask Jesus to help you feel His heart of love and delight in you. (Perhaps your heart will swell with joy, or you will feel light-headed with His peace and well-being)

4. Linger in this secret place with Jesus. If it's new for you, don't be surprised if your flesh fights it, or your mind brings distraction, for it can feel very vulnerable.

5. Thank Him for valuing you this much, and for the opportunity to bring Him joy.

Jesus' Words to You Today:

"My precious one, I have always loved you. You bring me so much joy in the process. Just you and me forever—what a delight! My love is simple, yet so profound. It is the very lifesource of your existence. The more you stay in this secret place, the more solid and secure you will be. Nothing will shake you and My love within you will overcome everything the enemy throws your way. You are My overcomer, My strong one, My redeemed one, My lover. My bride—how proud I am of you. :)"

- Day 30 -

WONDERFUL GRACE OF JESUS

"Finally, my beloved ones—may the wonderful grace of our Lord Jesus, the Anointed One, be flowing in your spirit. So shall it be!"
(Gal. 6:18, TPT)

What a glorious finish to this powerful letter! Everything mentioned in this letter—every word of correction and direction, transformation and assimilation is only made possible by the "wonderful grace of our Lord Jesus, the Anointed One." We can't change ourselves. We are powerless in our own might to walk out our faith in love without His grace. But through His grace, everything we inherit as His children is made possible.

Jesus Christ, the Anointed One, is our key. Anointing means, "rub, smear with oil." Jesus is smeared with oil (Holy Spirit), we are one with Him, and therefore we are also anointed. This anointing means we are set apart, sacred, empowered by Holy Spirit. His anointing releases the grace to accomplish all that He intended for us. His very presence and power flows through our spirit as we receive Him. His grace is a force pushing us forward toward more and more freedom and truth.

"So shall it be!" His promises are "yes and amen (so shall it be)." Once we truly understand the power of his grace and anointing in our lives, we can rejoice in our completeness in God. Col. 2:10 reaffirms, "...in Him you have been made complete, and He is the head over all rule and authority." (NASB) All we have to do is believe and participate in the work He is doing in and through us.

The author of Hebrews concludes with a similar declaration:

"...may he work perfection into every part of you giving you all that you need to fulfill your destiny. And may he express through you all that is excellent and pleasing to him through your life-union with Jesus the Anointed One who is to receive all glory forever!" (Heb. 13:21 TPT)

We will conclude this meditation of Galatians by giving Jesus, the Anointed One our gratitude:

Lord, thank you for choosing us as your bride, your loved ones.
Thank you for taking the punishment of our sins upon yourself.

...for sending the Holy Spirit to empower us to live righteously,

...for giving us love to flow through us to others

...for the promise of inheritance as God's dearly loved children,

...for freeing us from performance, religious duty and striving,

...for giving us dual citizenship in earth and heaven now,

...for taking away the long list of do's and don'ts,

...for showing us the beauty in ourselves and others,

...for directing us down a unique path, perfect for each one of us,

...for uniting us with a loving, powerful, heavenly Father.

We give you praise for all you've done and have yet to do. Glory to your Name!

Words from Holy Spirit:

"I have been sent to you while you are on earth to make you successful, empowered, able and willing to commune continually with your Father. I will work within you until you are a ready bride for His Son--spotless and wrinkle-free. I am proud to live inside you and to show you the Father's love. Let me take you into deeper waters. So much love...!"

Hidden Dove
by **ANN TUBBS**

DEVOTIONAL SERIES

About the Author

Ann was first a pastor's kid and then a pastor's wife for 24 years. Knowing there was more freedom available than she had known, God revealed an intimacy with Himself that she now shares around the world. She, and her husband Mark, have led nearly 100 mission trips to many nations. She also orchestrates 24-hour prayer strikes in strategic cities. Yet, her first love is to worship the Lord in heavenly places and enjoy His Presence. Now, she is sharing her revelations and experience with the Lord through this daily devotional in hopes that your relationship with God will go to greater height and depths.

| HIDDENDOVE.COM |
| TRANSFORMATIONOFTHENATIONS.COM |